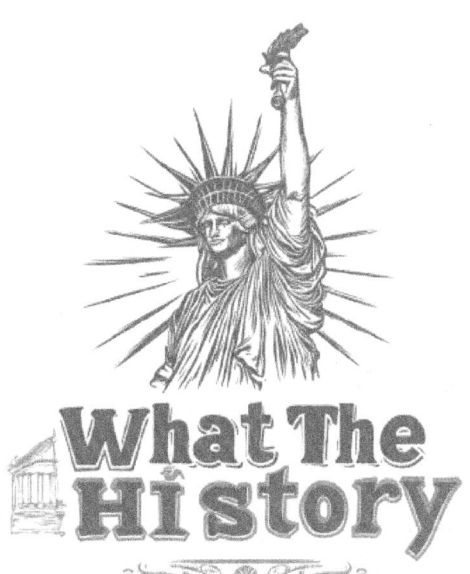

You are about to read the coolest History series ever written.

"Make History Wavy again"

THE CREATION OF ISRAEL

A New Nation Emerges in the Middle East

THE CREATION OF ISRAEL

Copyright © 2024 What The History

No part of this publication may be reproduced, stored in a retrieval system, or transmitted in any form or by any means, electronic, mechanical, photocopying, recording, or otherwise, without the prior written permission of the publisher.

Printed in the United States of America

First Edition: 2024

This copyright page includes the necessary copyright notice, permissions request information, acknowledgments for the cover design, interior design, and editing, as well as the details of the first edition.

www.littlebiggiant.com

Disclaimer: This book is a work of non-fiction and is intended for informational and educational purposes only. The names in this biography are trademarks of their respective owners. This book is not affiliated with, endorsed by, or sponsored by any of these trademark holders. The use of these names is intended solely to provide context and historical reference.

The author makes no claims to ownership of any trademarks or copyrights associated with the names and likenesses of the individuals referenced in this book. Any opinions expressed in this book are those of the author and do not reflect the views of any wrestling promotion or trademark holder.

Introduction

So, like, back in 1948, something super epic went down in the Middle East that totally changed history forever, ya know? After years of drama and hope, the Jewish peeps were like, "We're starting our own state!" and named it Israel. This wasn't just some random announcement; it was the result of, like, decades of struggle and dreams for a place to call home.

On May 14, when the sun was rising, everyone was watching as David Ben-Gurion, the first Prime Minister, was all like, "Boom! Israel is born!" and it sparked both celebrations and some serious tension. But, like, what actually led to this big moment? And what kinda challenges were waiting for this new nation? The answers are all mixed up in a wild story of history, filled with heroes, conflicts, and the never-ending search for peace.

The whole creation of Israel is just the start of a journey that still gets people talking and thinking all over the world. It's kinda lit, honestly!

Table of Contents

Table of Contents 7
Chapter 1 10
The Land of Milk and Honey 10
Chapter 2 18
A Dream of Home 18
Chapter 3 29
The Balfour Declaration 29
Chapter 4 37
The Struggles and Triumphs 37
Chapter 5 46
The United Nations and Partition 46
Chapter 6 55
The Declaration of Independence 55
Chapter 7 62
The War of Independence 62
Chapter 8 72

A Melting Pot of Cultures............................ 72
Chapter 9... **81**
Innovations and Inventions......................... 81
Chapter 10... **90**
The Ongoing Journey................................ 90

The Creation of Israel

Chapter 1

The Land of Milk and Honey

Yo, picture this: a super dope place that's like a treasure chest bursting with awesomeness. That's Israel, often dubbed the "Land of Milk and Honey." But like, what even does that mean? Let's throw it back in time and see why this land is so lit!

A long time ago, back in ancient days, folks thought Israel was a straight-up gift from the sky. The saying "Land of Milk and Honey" comes from the good old Bible, where it was said to be a place jam-packed with lush fields and epic views. Imagine rolling hills with cows just chilling, their milk helping everyone stay strong. Picture golden wheat fields waving in the breeze, and bees buzzing around flowers making that sweet, sweet honey. It was a place where people could totally live their best lives!

Israel's been the hangout for lots of different cultures and peeps throughout history. Think of a bustling marketplace with traders from all over, bringing their unique goods and crazy stories. There were ancient Israelites setting up cities and farms, and then the Romans came in, ruling the land and leaving behind some dope structures like the Western Wall, which is still iconic today. Every group that rolled through added to this rich history vibe.

Now, let's talk about why this land is a big deal. It's often called a crossroads of the world, where different cultures meet, kind of like the ultimate collab. Imagine standing on a hill, peeping out at the land, spotting mountains, valleys, and the super shiny Mediterranean Sea. This sick view has inspired artists, poets, and dreamers for ages. It's where tales of bravery, faith, and come-back energy have gone down.

One mega-important dude linked to this land is King David, who brought together the tribes of Israel and made Jerusalem his main spot. Imagine a young shepherd boy, all brave and stuff, who became a legendary king. He's remembered for his love of jamming and poetry, reminding us that even the littlest person can crush it.

As we dig deeper into the vibe of Israel, we gotta think about how it connects to our own journeys. Just like this land has been home to so many peeps, we all belong to our own communities. Each of us has a story to share, and together, we can totally make an epic narrative.

Israel is not just some dot on a map; it's a symbol of hope and strength. Throughout the years, peeps have faced some gnarly challenges, but they always found a way to band together and build a brighter future. The land schools us on the importance of unity and getting along with different cultures.

As we learn more about Israel, let's vibe on these questions: What can we learn from the stories of the people who called it home? How can we celebrate our differences and team up to make the world a better place?

Key Takeaway: Israel is like a rich tapestry of history and culture, reminding us that we're all connected, and together, we can totally make a rad future!

The Creation of Israel

Chapter 2

A Dream of Home

Once upon a time, like way back in the late 1800s, something super powerful started bubbling up in the hearts of Jewish folks everywhere. This was majorly about finding a place they could totally call home—a chill spot where they could live freely and practice their beliefs without freaking out. This vibe blossomed into what we now call the Zionist movement.

Picture a lively city packed with peeps from all kinds of backgrounds, right? Streets buzzing with laughter, music, and the mouthwatering smell of tasty food filling the air. But for many Jewish families in Eastern Europe, life was not all rainbows and sunshine. They were dealing with some serious hardships, discrimination, and sometimes bad stuff like violence. In this wild atmosphere of fear, a vision started to form—a wish to return to a land named Israel, a spot loaded with history and meaning for the Jewish people.

One of the big names who got the movement hyped was Theodor Herzl, a dude with a sparkle in his eye and loads of hope in his heart. This guy was a journalist who, after witnessing all the unfair treatment Jews got in Europe, was like, "Yo, we need a new plan!" He believed that if Jewish people could unite and chase one dream together, they could create a homeland for themselves. Herzl famously said, "If you will it, it is no dream." His words ignited a fire in many hearts, making them think their dream could actually happen, like, for real.

As Herzl's ideas spread like wildfire, more peeps jumped on the bandwagon. They held meetings, wrote letters, and gathered in groups, all buzzing about how to make this dream real. Imagine a room filled with passionate voices, everyone kinda sharing their hopes and fears, all in it together for the same cause. They saw a land where they could build schools, farms, and chill communities—a place where kids could run around under the sunny sky.

But, real talk, the road to making a homeland was not all smooth sailing. There were tons of challenges, and not everyone was vibing the same way. Some thought Jewish people should just make the best of where they were, while others were super keen about heading back to their historic homeland. These different views brought a drama kinda tension, like a tug-of-war between hearts and minds, y'know?

In 1897, the first Zionist Congress kicked off in Switzerland, where folks from all over rolled in to talk about their plans. Picture it—a grand hall packed with excited faces, the air buzzing with anticipation. Together, they started crafting a plan to get Jewish people to settle in Palestine, the land they believed was rightfully theirs. They were all about creating a place where Jewish culture could blossom, just like flowers coming alive after a long, harsh winter.

As this movement picked up steam, so did the dreams of many. Families started packing their bags, leaving their old lives behind in search of something new. They journeyed across oceans, facing the unknown with mad courage. They hoped to build a community where they could raise their kids, pass down their traditions, and live in peace like a big happy family.

But this journey wasn't just about finding a crib; it was also about figuring out identity and belonging. As Jewish peeps began to settle in Palestine, they faced a whole new set of challenges. They had to learn to work the land, build homes, and start from scratch, like serious ground-up vibes. Imagine the sounds of hammers hitting nails, the smell of fresh earth, and kids laughing as families teamed up to create their dreams.

The Zionist movement was more than just a wish; it became this strong force connecting Jewish people worldwide. It showed them they weren't alone; they were part of a bigger story—a story of hope, resilience, and the quest to belong, for real though.

As we look back at this bit of history, we get reminded of just how powerful dreams can be and the importance of coming together for something greater. The Zionist movement sparked a global convo about identity, home, and the right to live in peace. It teaches us that no matter how far apart we seem, we're all linked by our hopes and dreams—like, always.

Key Takeaway: Dreams can totally bring people together and inspire them to hustle for a common goal, even when times get tough. Just like the Zionist movement, let's all strive to create a better world by believing in our dreams and having each other's backs.

The Creation of Israel

Chapter 3

The Balfour Declaration

Back in the early 20th century, something major went down that totally flipped the script for a lot of people. This moment was all wrapped up in a letter—yeah, you heard that right—a letter! Known as the Balfour

Declaration, this piece of paper was named after Arthur Balfour, the British Foreign Secretary at the time, and let me tell you, it was heavy with hope, dreams, but also a whole bunch of conflict and uncertainty.

Picture an old-school library, like something out of a movie, with dusty books and that old-paper smell in the air. In one corner, a squad of dudes was huddled around a massive wooden table, looking dead serious. They were deep in convo about a land called Palestine, which held mad history and meaning for both Jews and Arabs. The year was 1917, and let's keep it real—World War I had everyone on edge, nations were battling it out, and folks were just trying to find somewhere to call home, ya know?

In this tense vibe, Balfour shot off a letter to a Jewish leader named Lord Rothschild. The letter was lit—it said the British government was down for a "national home for the Jewish people" in Palestine. Simple words but it was like fireworks going off in history! For Jews, this was a huge hope after being bullied and discriminated against for ages. They were dreaming of hitting up the land where their ancestors came from so they could rebuild their lives and fams.

But hold up, what about the Arab folks already living in Palestine? They had mad ties to that land, living there for generations and whatnot. The whole Balfour situation stirred the pot, causing anxiety and fears among the Arabs about what this new support meant for their future. Would they still fit in the picture of the land they called home? Yeah, things were about to get real complicated!

As the word about the Balfour Declaration spread like wildfire, it sparked a serious hope wave among Jews globally. They were straight-up celebrating and starting to dream of a future where they could chill freely in their homeland. But don't get it twisted—this also got the Arab community riled up, feeling like they were being ignored. This growing tension was just the beginning of a long and wild ride for both groups.

The Balfour Declaration became more than just a legal doc; it morphed into a symbol of all kinds of dreams that were somehow at odds. Over the years, it led to some huge moments, like the setting up of the State of Israel in 1948, which had people feeling a mix of joy and sadness. For many Jews, it was like finally scoring their big dream; but for a whole lot of Arabs, it kicked off a painful chapter they didn't ask for.

Amid all this, we gotta think—what does it even mean to belong somewhere? How do we juggle our hopes with those of other people? The Balfour Declaration is a solid reminder that history is like a wild mix tape, full of different stories, each representing the hopes and fears of all kinds of communities. It pushes us to think about how our choices now can totally affect other peeps' lives later.

Key Takeaway: The Balfour Declaration shows that words can legit change the game in history, and we should always be here for the dreams of everyone, 'cause we're all sharing this world together.

The Creation of Israel

Chapter 4

The Struggles and Triumphs

So, once upon a time in this epic land that was like, totally filled with ancient stones and echoing history, a brave crew of dudes and dudettes set out to make a sweet new home. They were known as the early settlers of Israel, and their story is like, honestly a mix of major struggles and some insane triumphs. Just picture it: the sun peeking over the hills, spilling golden vibes on the dusty roads, while all around you there's that perf smell of blooming flowers. But lemme tell ya, this land wasn't just all pretty; it was also crazy tough!

When those early settlers rolled up, they were hit with hella challenges. The land was all dry and rocky, like some bad scene from a movie, and they had to flip it into fertile fields ready for crops to grow. Imagine just standing there in what feels like a massive desert, with only a few scraggly plants and the scorching sun beating down. It's like trying to build a sandcastle at the beach but it just keeps washing away, ya know? But these settlers were super determined. They got their hands dirty, digging and planting, holding on to the hope for a bountiful harvest.

There was one iconic figure among these settlers: David Ben-Gurion. This guy was like a total boss, steering a ship through mega stormy seas. He was all about that dream of a Jewish homeland and inspired others to jump on the bandwagon with him. He'd gather folks around, sharing stories that lit up their hearts like fireworks on the Fourth of July, and painted this dope picture of a thriving community. It was like he had a magic touch, sparking the passion to build a brighter future.

But let's be real, the grind wasn't easy. The settlers faced not just the tough nature stuff but also the drama of living together in this new spot. They had to get it together, work as a squad, and support each other like a team of superheroes. Picture a group of besties, each with their own epic skills, teaming up to tackle problems. Like, one buddy is a pro at planting seeds, while another can whip up some sturdy houses. Together, they built a strong community that was united by their dreams and mad determination.

But hold up! Their struggles weren't done yet. There were beefs with neighboring communities, all trying to stake their claim in the land. It was basically a tug-of-war, with both sides pulling in totally different directions. The settlers had to walk a fine line, seeking peace while clinging to their dream of a homeland. They learned that sometimes, building a new life takes patience and understanding, like planting seeds and chillin' while waiting for them to bloom.

As time went on, the hustle started to pay off, fam. Fields that were once a total wasteland evolved into vibrant patches of green, bursting with fruits and veggies. It was nothing short of a miracle! The settlers threw major celebrations, full of laughter and joy, feasting on meals whipped up from their own harvest. They even built schools for their kiddos, turning knowledge into gold like the crops in their fields. They weren't just getting by—they were living their best lives!

But the story? Oh, it keeps going! With every win, new challenges popped up like whack-a-mole. As the settlers were busy building their new life, they came to realize they had to defend their dreams, too. They learned how to be resilient, standing tall like mighty trees in a storm and refusing to be uprooted. They figured out that even when times got rough, they had the strength to keep pushing.

So, if there's one thing we can snag from the struggles and wins of these early settlers, it's this: Determination, teamwork, and just a sprinkle of hope can help us crush even the wildest challenges. Just like these settlers flipped dry land into flourishing fields, we can totally turn our dreams into reality, no matter how impossible they seem at first.

Key Takeaway: When challenges hit, hard work and team spirit can totally help us build a brighter future! ✨

The Creation of Israel

Chapter 5

The United Nations and Partition

So, like, once upon a time, right after World War II, the whole world was pumped about peace and stuff. Everyone was daydreaming about a better future, where everyone could just chill and live in harmony. But, over in a lil corner of the world, there was some seriously major talk happening. It was all about this land called Palestine, where Jewish and Arab people had been living for ages. This land was super important for both groups, but it was also, like, a total hotspot of conflict.

As the sun dipped below the horizon, painting everything in this warm golden vibe, a squad of leaders from all over the planet came together in this fancy building called the United Nations. Picture this big ol' room filled with folks from everywhere, each with their own stories and dreams. It was kinda like a superhero team, each person bringing their own special abilities to tackle a huge problem. Their mission? To figure out how Jewish folks, who'd faced major struggles during the war, and Arab folks, who had their own dreams for the area, could somehow get along.

Then in 1947, after lots of talking and maybe a bit of arguing, the United Nations dropped a bold plan known as the Partition Plan. Imagine a giant cake, and the UN was trying to slice it into two equal pieces. One piece was meant for the Jewish people, and the other for the Arab folks. The plan said the land would be split into two separate states, and Jerusalem, this city that was super sacred to both sides, would be an international city for everyone.

But, like, not everyone was stoked about this plan. The Jewish community, who had been wishing for a place to call their own, felt a spark of hope flickering. They saw this as a shot to create a safe haven where they could vibe and celebrate their culture. But a bunch of Arab leaders were concerned. They thought the plan was super unfair and that they'd be losing their land. It was kinda like sharing a favorite toy with a friend who didn't wanna play nice at all.

As word spread, excitement mixed with fear in the air. Both sides were feeling some hardcore emotions. Imagine families, all on edge, chatting about their future. Would they be able to coexist peacefully, or were they doomed for some serious drama?

When the United Nations voted on the Partition Plan, it passed! The excitement was lit. Jewish communities were throwing parties, while Arab communities were feeling mad and sad. The whole world was, like, glued to the scene, kinda like a crowd at an epic sports game, waiting for the next big play.

But hold up, that wasn't the end. The announcement sparked protests and chaos. Misunderstandings and fears blew up, and people started picking sides. The dream of peace was slipping away, man. Things got messy, and tensions started simmering even more.

Amidst all this craziness, the UN leaders were still grinding away. They really wanted to bring everyone together and work towards a peaceful solution. They were, like, a group of wise owls navigating through a dark forest. But finding the right path was no walk in the park; challenges were everywhere.

As time passed, the world was watching with fingers crossed. Could the Jewish and Arab people figure out how to live side by side? Or would their differences just turn into more chaos? It was still a mystery hanging in the air, like a cliffhanger episode of your favorite show.

Key Takeaway: The creation of Israel was a wild and emotional journey, filled with tons of voices and viewpoints. It reminds us how crucial it is to listen to one another, understand diverse perspectives, and work together to find peaceful solutions. Just like in a big squad, every voice matters, and together we can craft a totally awesome future!

The Creation of Israel

Chapter 6

The Declaration of Independence

Back in spring of '48, like, you could feel the buzz in the air, kinda like the hype before an epic concert. The world was about to change big time, and in this lil room in Tel

Aviv, history was about to go down. Picture a squad of super driven folks, each holdin' onto their dreams like they were precious gems. They were all about hope and courage, just wanting a place to finally call home.

So, this was when the Declaration of Independence for Israel got its start. Imagine a sunny day in May, with the sun beaming down on the busy city, and everyone totally buzzing with excitement. In that room, the Jewish community's leaders were all gathered, their hearts racing like they'd just seen their fave band walk in. And there was David

Ben-Gurion, this tall dude with a serious vibe, who was soon gonna be Israel's first Prime Minister.

When he stood up to talk, it was like someone hit pause on everything. The room was dead silent. Ben-Gurion's voice was strong and filled with passion. He went on about the crazy struggles the Jewish people had faced and their dreams for a safe space after going through so much. He described Israel as a land full of their history and culture, like a treasure waiting to be found.

Every word he said was super electrifying! The declaration was not just some piece of paper, but a total promise, a light in the dark for everyone who had waited so long for peace. When he proclaimed, "We hereby declare the establishment of the Jewish state in the land of Israel," it felt like a wave of happiness crashed over the room. People hugged, cheered, and there's no doubt some tears were shed. They'd waited ages for this, and it was finally happening!

But it wasn't all rainbows and butterflies. Outside, the world was totally watching. The declaration was like a lil spark in a dark room, lighting up the way ahead but also raising big questions. What would come next? Would all these dreams of peace actually happen, or were rough times ahead?

So, May 14, '48, marked the day Israel was officially born—it was like a moment that would flip the history script. It was when dreams took off, like birds soaring high in the sky, bringing with 'em the hopes of an entire nation.

As the sun dipped that historic day, Israel's first flag was raised, those blue and white colors dancing in the wind. It stood for a fresh start, a new identity, and a home where folks could just vibe and live with dignity. The night sky was shining with stars, each one kinda reminding everyone of the dreams that came true and all the ones still waiting to happen.

In the years to come, the journey wouldn't always be a piece of cake, there would be bumps in the road. But that day's spirit—like the hype, the hope, and that unstoppable drive—would continue to motivate countless generations.

Key Takeaway: The Declaration of Independence for Israel shows us that hope and determination can totally change the game. Just like the people in that room back in '48, we all have the power to dream big and hustle hard to make those dreams a reality, like the true legends we are!

Chapter 7

The War of Independence

Back in the early 1900s, a dream started to form in the hearts of lots of Jewish folks: they wanted a homeland, a place where they could chill and call it their own, ya know? This dream sparked a big struggle called the War of Independence. Just imagine a massive landscape with rolling hills and ancient cities, where all sorts of people were living together, but things were getting tense—like, real stormy vibes were brewing, for real.

So, on May 14, 1948, as the sun was peeking out, the atmosphere was supercharged with excitement. David Ben-Gurion, a totally passionate dude, stood in front of a crowd in Tel Aviv, announcing that the State of Israel was officially a thing! It was a major moment for many people, but hold up—it also kicked off a pretty rough journey. Almost right away, neighboring countries freaked out and thought they were threatened. They were seriously not ready to accept this whole Jewish homeland idea.

Picture this: families huddled in their living rooms, tuned into the radio, hearts racing with a mix of hope and worry. The news spread faster than wildfire, and soon, armies from Egypt, Jordan, Syria, Lebanon, and Iraq were gearing up to invade. It was like watching a huge wave crash into a delicate sandcastle.

This young state of Israel, barely a few hours old, was suddenly in a Fight Club for its life.

The War of Independence wasn't just a bunch of soldiers throwing down; it was like a showdown of hopes and dreams. On one side, you had the Israelis, trying to stand their ground, while on the flip side were the Arab armies, wanting to crush the whole Israel vibe. The battles were intense, with both sides having moments of bravery mixed with heartbreak. Villages got attacked, and a ton of people were forced to flee, creating a massive feeling of loss that stuck around for ages.

One of the wildest battles went down in Jerusalem—a city that's sacred to a lot of folks. A total scene, right? Narrow streets filled with foot stomps, people shouting, and tanks rumbling nearby. This city was a beacon of hope and faith, and both sides were itching to claim it. The fighting here was brutal, with soldiers and civilians caught in the chaos. It was a time when bravery was tested, and unexpected friendships sprang up right ducking in the heat of battle.

While the war was spilling over, the whole world was watching this drama with bated breath. News reporters painted crazy vivid pictures of what was happening, and people everywhere felt the stakes rising. Many Jewish folks far away felt a strong connection to what was going down in Israel. They wrote letters, sent cash, and even volunteered to back up the new state. It was like, community goals, y'know?

Even with all the hardships, the Israeli spirit was shining bright, fam. They united, working non-stop to build their nation amidst all this chaos. Farmers were working their fields, teachers were shaping the next gen, and artists were crafting dope pieces that showed their hopes and dreams. For real, their resilience was like a light in the darkness, keeping everyone hyped.

As the war trudged on, something epic happened. The Israeli forces started gaining traction, pushing back the invading armies bit by bit. Small victories were like a slowly rising tide, and they began securing their territory. The war was brutal and long, but the people's determination was lit. They weren't just fighting for land; they were fighting for the right to exist, to thrive, and to build a future for their kiddos.

By the time the dust settled in 1949, Israel was officially a new nation—though it came at a heavy price. Thousands had lost their lives, and families were torn apart a ton. The scars of war were deep, creating a complex web of emotions—grief, pride, and hope mixed together like a crazy smoothie. The boundaries of this fresh state were drawn, but the drama and challenges were just getting started.

The War of Independence totally shaped Israel's future, setting the stage for all the awesome struggles and achievements that lay ahead. It was a wild time of change, where dreams slammed into reality, and the people's resilience was put through the wringer. Looking back on this chapter, it reminds us of the power of hope and how important it is to understand each other.

Key Takeaway: The War of Independence shows us that chasing our dreams can be super tough, but it also reveals the strength that comes when we unite and stay strong through the gritty times. For real!

CHAPTER 8

A Melting Pot of Cultures

In the heart of the Middle East, there's this tiny but totally amazing country called Israel. It's like a place where history is like, whisperin' through the wind, and cultures mix together like a super cool paint job. Picture this: you're in a bustling market, the air smells sweet like all those spices, and crazy bright fruits and veggies are everywhere. This is what Israel's all about—a wild mashup of cultures, traditions, and epic stories just waiting for you to check 'em out.

As you wander 'round the streets of Jerusalem, you can hear soft prayers from all sorts of faiths blending together like it's one awesome song. You got ancient buildings chillin' next to modern architecture, each one telling its own story. The Western Wall, which is super sacred for Jews, is super close to the Church of the Holy Sepulchre, where Christians believe Jesus got that whole buried thing going on. And don't sleep on the Al-Aqsa Mosque! It's one of the holiest spots in Islam and it's reaching for the sky like "Check me out!" It's like time woven these different threads into a fab tapestry that shows off the rich history of the land.

In Israel, you're gonna meet a ton of different peeps. There's Jewish families that came from places like Europe, North Africa, and even Ethiopia, bringing their own wild customs and delish recipes. Just imagine a table piled with golden-brown falafel, warm pita bread, and sticky sweet baklava. Each bite is like a time travel adventure through people's stories. Yum, right?

But hold up, it's not only the Jewish culture that's poppin'. The Arab community plays a mad important role in our vibrant society too. In towns like Nazareth, you can catch the sounds of Arabic music filling the streets, just begging for you to dance and celebrate. Festivals like Eid al-Fitr and Ramadan are totally celebrated with a ton of joy, showing how family and community are everything here. All these different cultures creating a fab mosaic where traditions are shared and friendships grow is just lit.

Oh, and let's not forget about the Druze! They're a dope, unique religious group with their own customs and beliefs. Known for their bravery and loyalty, they're all in with serving in the Israeli army and helping keep the country safe. When they celebrate their own festivals, you'll see colorful dances and tasty foods that make their mark on Israel's cultural scene.

Head farther north to the Galilee, and you'll find the Baha'i Gardens, a jaw-dropping example of beauty and chill vibes. These gardens symbolize unity and peace, like a reminder that even though we're all different, we can come together to create some seriously amazing stuff. As you stroll through the perfectly groomed paths, you might just find yourself thinkin': How can we, like these flowers, bloom together in harmony?

The arts are also thriving here, with musicians, dancers, and artists bringing their diverse identities to life through their work. Imagine a theater filled with laughter as actors tell stories that reflect the many lives in Israel. Every show is like a party of culture, reminding us that despite our differences, our feels and dreams totally connect us.

When the sun starts to dip below the Mediterranean, painting the sky with those crazy orange and pink vibes, the people of Israel come together for family dinners, sharing stories and laughs. They celebrate what makes them different, knowing it's those differences that really make their country shine.

So, in Israel, the past, present, and future are like dancing stars in the night sky, creating this cosmic ballet of cultures. Everyone adds their own flavor to this land, making it a living, breathing community bursting with stories, laughter, and love.

Key Takeaway: Think of Israel like a colorful salad packed with all different ingredients. Its beauty comes from the variety of cultures and communities. Embrace our differences, and we'll totally learn from one another, creating a stronger and more vibrant world! How awesome is that?

Chapter 9

Innovations and Inventions

So, once upon a time, in a place full of ancient vibes and rad cultures, a teeny-tiny country called Israel kinda popped up as this mega hotspot for creativity and invention. Picture this! A buzzing workshop where total genius peeps come together, all hyped to solve big issues and make the world way better. That's Israel for ya—like a land where inventiveness just vibes with the sunshine chillin' in the clear blue sky.

In the core of Israel, a squad of young scientists and engineers gathered to tackle one of the most epic challenges of our time: water scarcity. Like, Israel has to be real smart about how it uses water since it doesn't have as much as other places do. So, they whipped up this super cool tech called drip irrigation! Imagine a tiny water droplet giving life to plants right where they grow, kinda like how a mom looks after her kid. This method doesn't just save water but also helps farmers crank out more food in a fraction of the space. Today, this dope technique is used everywhere, helping feed tons of people.

But wait, there's more! Israel also rocks some of the most advanced medical tech out there. Like, consider doctors trying to save lives. Wouldn't it be lit if they could peek inside someone's body without all the pain? Thanks to some Israeli inventors, we've got this wild thing called a "pill camera." It's a teeny camera that you can just swallow like a regular pill! Once it's in there, it snaps pics of your insides while it journeys through your belly, sending all the intel back to the doctor. This invention is like having a superhero chillin' in your stomach, helping docs understand what's up without any of that cringe-worthy stuff.

As we cruise through this land of innovation, we gotta shout out the insane contributions to tech too! Ever used a smartphone? Well, guess what? A bunch of the apps and tech we use every day were cooked up by Israeli companies! For instance, the super popular messaging app WhatsApp was dreamt up by two Israeli entrepreneurs! Just imagine sending a message to your friend in a flash, no matter where they are across the globe. It's like having a magical phone that connects us all, no cap!

Israel is also killing it in renewable energy. Picture the sun beaming down on a field of shiny solar panels, just soaking up all that good sunlight like it's a sponge. These panels grab the sun's energy and flip it into electricity, powering homes and schools. This is not just solid for the planet; it's like giving Mother Earth a sweet gift, making sure we have clean energy for ages to come.

As we dive into these inventions, we can't help but wonder: What sparks people to create such rad things? Maybe it's all about curiosity and wanting to level up the world. Just like the inventors in Israel, we've all got the power to dream big and think outside the box. Whether it's building a robot, designing a fire game, or finding a way to help others, each one of us can be an innovator in our own epic way.

In the end, the saga of Israel's innovations is not just about tech; it's about peeps—those who dare to dream, create, and change the world. As we look to the future, let's keep that spirit of innovation alive in our hearts, ready to tackle challenges and make a solid difference.

Key Takeaway: Innovation comes from being curious and wanting to solve problems. Just like the inventors in Israel, we can all think creatively and make the world a way better place!

The Creation of Israel

Chapter 10

The Ongoing Journey

In the heart of the Middle East, where the sun totally vibes with the earth and the winds spill ancient tea, there's this place called Israel. It's a land packed with hope but also struggles, a place where history and today do this wild dance, kinda like a spider weaving its web but as delicate as a butterfly flipping 'round.

Picture this: you're standing on a hill, peeping at the bustling city of Jerusalem, where the shiny Dome of the Rock is basically glowing in the sunlight. You got people from all backgrounds—Jews, Muslims, and Christians—coming together to pray, remember stuff, and dream about a better future. But it's not all sunshine and rainbows. This place has had its share of drama and conflict, like a cool painting splashed with some dark colors.

The journey to peace in Israel is a lot like a twisty river. Sometimes it flows super smooth, but then it hits rocks and sticks and gets all blocked up. For years, folks have been trying to find a way to live together all chill and peaceful, but misunderstandings and arguments often throw a wrench in it. Imagine trying to build a bridge and the blocks just keep tumbling down; that's kinda how tough it can be to find some common ground.

Right now, looking at the issues, people in Israel and Palestine got a whole bunch of hurdles to jump over. They argue about land, safety, and everyone just wanting to live their lives freely. Kids—just like you—dream about playing in parks without worries, hitting up school with no fear, and making friends from different backgrounds. But a lot of kiddos in this area grow up hearing way more conflict stories than laughter.

But hold up! There's still hope! Like flowers popping after a rainstorm, loads of people are hustling to spread peace. Organizations and folks are reaching out, telling stories, and trying to listen to each other. Think of a squad of kids from various neighborhoods coming together to shoot some hoops, laughing and cheering for each other. That's the kind of unity many are dreaming about in Israel.

Looking back through history, you see both leaders and everyday heroes trying to build bridges of understanding. You hear stories about brave peeps standing up for peace, refusing to slide into anger and hate. These legends remind us that, even in the darkest times, one little candle can totally light up an entire room.

As we think about what's next, let's ask ourselves: What can we do to help? How can we be part of the solution? The road to peace is ongoing, needing all of us to be brave, kind, and ready to listen. Just like those stars sparkling in the night sky, every person can shine bright and make a difference.

In this epic tapestry of life, we gotta remember that every thread counts. The future of Israel and its peeps isn't just hanging on the big shots but on the hearts of everyone who's dreaming of a brighter tomorrow. So, let's vibe together about a world where kids get to grow up in peace, where laughter fills the air, and where each new day brings in a wave of hope.

Key Takeaway: Peace is a journey that needs understanding, compassion, and teamwork. Just like in the best game ever, each of us has a part to play in making a brighter future for everyone. 🌟

The Creation of Israel

The Creation of Israel

Dear Cool Kids/Parents

Thank you for choosing "What the History"! We hope this book has ignited a spark of wonder and motivation within you.

If you found this book captivating and believe in the transformative power of its message, we kindly ask for your support. Please consider leaving a glowing review on the platform where you purchased the book. Your review will help spread this message of empowerment to even more young readers, inspiring them to dream big and reach for the stars.

The core essence of this book - to inspire and uplift young minds - is what truly matters. We acknowledge that perfection is elusive, and we appreciate your understanding and forgiveness for any minor imperfections.

Thank you for being a part of our mission to nurture the brilliance and potential within the next generation. Your feedback will go a long way in helping us continue to provide captivating and transformative stories for young readers.